W9-BZO-558

Looking at Weather

David Suzuki

with BARBARA HEHNER

John Wiley & Sons, Inc.
New York • Chichester • Brisbane • Toronto • Singapore

j551.5
S968L
c.1

In recognition of the importance of preserving what has been written, it is a policy of John Wiley & Sons, Inc., to have books of enduring value published in the United States printed on acid-free paper, and we exert our best efforts to that end.

Copyright © 1988, 1991 by New Data Enterprises and Barbara Hehner.

Published in Canada by Stoddart Publishing Co., Limited
First U.S. edition published by John Wiley & Sons, Inc., in 1991
Illustrations © 1987, 1991 by Oni.

This publication is designed to provide accurate and authoritative information in regard to the subject matter covered. It is sold with the understanding that the publisher is not engaged in rendering legal, accounting, or other professional service. If legal advice or other expert assistance is required, the services of a competent professional person should be sought. From a Declaration of Principles jointly adopted by a Committee of the American Bar Association and a Committee of Publishers.

Library of Congress Cataloging-in-Publication Data

Suzuki, David T., 1936–
    Looking at weather / David Suzuki ; with Barbara Hehner.
      p.   cm. — *(David Suzuki's Looking at Series)*
    Includes index.
    Summary: Describes the changes in weather, how weather affects people's lives, and how people affect weather. Includes activities.
    ISBN 0-471-54753-0 (lib. edition). — ISBN 0-471-54047-1 (paper)
    1. Weather—Juvenile literature. [1. Weather.]
I. Hehner, Barbara. II. Title.
QC981.3.S89   1991
551.5—dc20   91-9258
                           AC

Printed in the United States of America

10 9 8 7 6 5 4 3 2 1

The publisher and the author have made every reasonable effort to ensure that the experiments and activities in this book are safe when conducted as instructed but assume no responsibility for any damage caused or sustained while performing the experiments or activities in Looking at Weather. Parents, guardians, and/or teachers should supervise young readers who undertake the experiments and activities in this book.

All rights reserved.

Reproduction or translation of any part of this work beyond that permitted by section 107 or 108 of the 1976 United States Copyright Act without the permission of the copyright owner is unlawful. Requests for permission or further information should be addressed to the Permission Department, John Wiley & Sons, Inc.

CHICAGO HEIGHTS PUBLIC LIBRARY

Table of Contents

AN IMPORTANT NOTE FOR KIDS AND GROWNUPS
You will see this (✋) warning sign on some of the **Things to Do** in this book. It means that an adult should help out. The project may use some boiling water or something might need to be cut with a knife. Everyone needs to be extra careful. Most grownups will want to get involved in these projects anyway—why should kids have all the fun?

Introduction

Don't you love the way our weather changes as the seasons change? The weather reminds me of how all things on Earth are linked together. Clouds are made from water that evaporated from lakes and oceans and from water that was sucked up by the roots of plants and breathed out from their leaves. The air is freshened by great forests, which take in carbon dioxide and give back oxygen. Energy from the sun makes all life on Earth possible. All of these things — sun, air, water — go into making up our weather.

As I travel around the world, I am always being surprised by the weather. Once, in the far north, it was so cold that when I breathed out, I could hear the tinkle of ice crystals forming as my breath froze. Another time, I was in a Pakistan desert when the temperature was 122°F (50°C). I felt as if I were baking in an oven!

Do you ever wonder what causes changes in weather? How does weather affect people's lives — and how do people affect the weather? These are some of the interesting questions we'll explore in this book.

DAVID SUZUKI

What Makes Weather?

It All Starts with the Sun

What's weather? Weather is the wind in your face when you run. It's rain and clouds and sunshine. It's heat that makes you sweaty, and cold that stings your cheeks and numbs your toes.

Weather plays a big part in your life, every day of the year. What clothes are you wearing today? Shorts and a T-shirt? A warm jacket? You have to dress for the weather. Will you be able to build a snowfort after school? Can you have a picnic in the park on Saturday? That depends on the weather.

People may not know whether it will rain tomorrow. But they know, in a general way, what kind of weather they can expect at different times of the year. The usual kind of weather a place has is called its *climate*. If you look through a picture book about other countries, you can see how people choose their clothes and build their houses to suit the climate. In the Swiss Alps, for instance, many houses have steep roofs so that heavy snowfalls can slide to the ground.

Why is it, though, that different places in the world have such different weather? And why does the weather change from season to season? The Earth's weather story really starts a long way away from our planet—in fact, about 92,000,000 miles (148,000,000 km) away. That's the distance from the Earth to the Sun.

The Sun is a huge, churning ball of exploding gases. The explosions cause the Sun to *radiate* (send out) enormous amounts of energy. Some of this energy reaches the Earth, where it's turned into heat. Some parts of the Earth are heated much more than others, though. Why?

Have a look at a globe, a model of the Earth. Around the middle of the globe is an imaginary line called the *Equator*. While the Earth goes around and around the Sun, the Sun shines almost straight at the Equator. But at the North and South Poles, the Sun's rays hit the Earth at a big slant. At this angle, the Sun's rays can't warm the earth nearly as much. So the Polar regions are much colder than the Tropics (the areas near the E-quator).

There's something else to notice about a globe. It sits in its frame at an angle. This is to show that the Earth is tipped as it goes around the Sun. For half the year, the Northern Hemisphere (the top half of the globe) is tilted toward the Sun. It receives more heat at this time, and summer comes to North America. For the other half of the year, the Northern Hemisphere is tilted away from the Sun. This is when North America has winter, with less heat coming from the Sun. As you can figure out, the Southern Hemisphere has to be tilted toward the Sun while the Northern Hemisphere is tilted away. So it's summer in Australia when it's winter in North America.

Now you know something about why some places are colder than others. To go any further with the weather story, though, you have to look much closer to Earth than the Sun. Rain, snow, clouds, and winds are all forming just a few kilometres above your head, in the Earth's *atmosphere*. That's what the rest of this book is about.

Color Me Cool

Did you know that the color of your clothes can make you feel hotter or cooler on a sizzling summer day? Find out why.

What You Need:
two outdoor or room thermometers
some sheets of paper in different
    colors, including black and white
    sheets—all the same size
    and thickness

a sunny summer day

What to Do:
1. Place the two thermometers outside in a shady place. What is the temperature? Write it down and save it. This is the air temperature.

2. Now put the two thermometers in the sun. Cover one thermometer with a sheet of white paper. Cover the other one with a sheet of black paper. Leave them in the sun for about half an hour.

3. Take off the sheets of paper and see what the thermometers say.

Under which sheet of paper was it hotter? On a hot summer day, do you think it would be better to wear a white T-shirt or a black one?

4. Try this test again with other colors of paper.

What's Happening?
Dark-colored things are able to soak up sunlight and turn it into heat. Light-colored things are more likely to reflect the heat without heating up. As you learned earlier in the book, the sun's rays hit the North and South Poles at a big slant. There's another reason why the poles stay so cold, though. They're covered by white snow, which reflects the sun's rays without heating the ground below.

Sunshine Sizzler

With a solar cooker, you can use the sun's rays to cook yourself a hotdog. Ask a grownup to help you with this big project.

What You Need:
sheets of cardboard, thin enough
    to cut with scissors
scissors
pencil and ruler
a cardboard carton
a shish-kebab skewer or other piece of
    wire (an unpainted, straightened-
    out coat-hanger will do)
aluminum foil
rubber cement
clear sticky tape
2 bolts and 2 wing nuts

a hot summer day

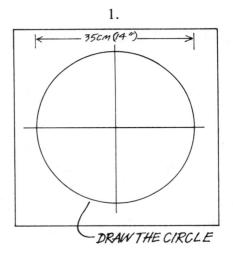

1.

35cm (14")

DRAW THE CIRCLE

What to Do:

1. On pieces of cardboard, draw two circles that are 14 inches (35 cm) in diameter. (Do you know what the diameter of a circle is? It's a straight line that goes right across the circle, passing through the center.)

2. Now draw two straight lines to divide each circle into four equal sections. (See Drawing 1.)

3. On one line, mark an x halfway between the center and each edge of the circle, as shown in Drawing 2.

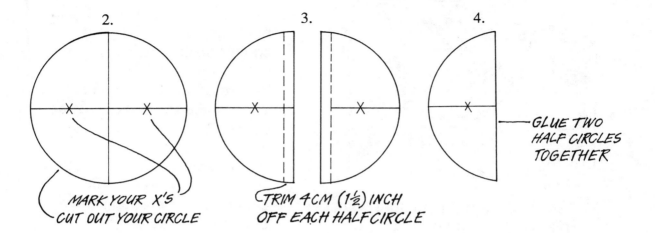

2. MARK YOUR X'S
CUT OUT YOUR CIRCLE

3. TRIM 4 CM (1½) INCH
OFF EACH HALF CIRCLE

4. GLUE TWO
HALF CIRCLES
TOGETHER

4. Cut along the other line to divide each circle in halves. Then trim a piece 1½ inches (4 cm) wide from each half circle. (See Drawing 3.)

5. Glue two half circles together with rubber cement to make your cooker stronger. Do the same with the other two half circles.

6. Cut a piece of cardboard 10 inches by 20 inches (25 cm by 50 cm). Cover one side of this cardboard with aluminum foil, shiny side out.

7. This is a bit tricky. Tape the *long edges* of the cardboard piece to the *curved* edges of the two half circles. The idea is to gently coax the cardboard piece into a rounded shape without making any fold lines across it. (See Drawing 5.)

8. Poke holes through the end pieces of your solar cooker, where you marked x in step 3. When you're ready to cook a wiener, the skewer will stretch across between these holes.

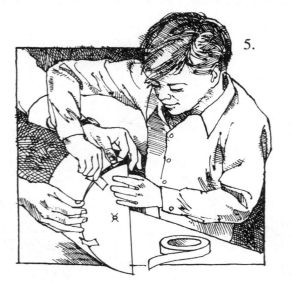

5.

10. *Plan* the next step before you make any holes. Set your cooker inside the frame, so that its opening faces out. You're going to put holes through the two side walls of the cooker and the two side walls of the frame. Then you're going to use the bolts and wing nuts to join the cooker and frame, as shown in Drawing 7. You want the cooker to be able to swing freely inside the frame, so that you can tilt it to get the most sun possible. When you've got this figured out, poke holes and attach the bolts.

9. Now make a frame to hold your solar cooker. You need a cardboard carton that is just a little bigger than your cooker. Cut the top and front from the box as shown in Drawing 6.

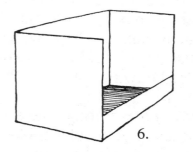

6.

7.

11. The best time to use your cooker is at noon on a hot summer day. Put a wiener on the skewer. Tilt the cooker so that sun is reflected on the wiener. Now sit back and let the sun do the rest. It will take about 20 minutes to cook a wiener. Turn it once while it's cooking. Yummy!

• This cooker is based on a design by Jesse Slome, Energy Workshop.

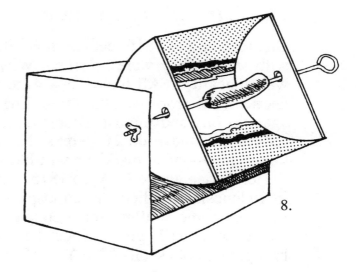

8.

AMAZING FACTS

Hot Enough for You?

The highest air temperature ever recorded on Earth was 136.4°F (58.0°C). The place was Al'azizyah, Libya, on September 22, 1922. The hottest place in North America is Death Valley, California, which reached 134°F (56.7°C) on July 10, 1913. The lowest reading we have is for Vostok, Antarctica. The temperature there plunged to -128.6°F (-89.2°C) on July 21, 1983. (Remember, July is the middle of winter in the Southern Hemisphere!) Canada holds the North American record. It was -81.4° F (-63.0°C) at Snag, Yukon, on February 3, 1947. Most people would be happy to stay away from such places while they're setting records. Yet Earth is a gentle planet compared with its closest neighbors. Temperatures on Mars can be as low as -193°F (-125°C), while Venus sizzles at 864°F (462°C).

The Year Without a Summer

One morning in 1816, people in Halifax awoke to find the ground covered with snow. They were horrified. Why? It was June, a month when snow was unheard of. All their crops were ruined. From Quebec down to Connecticut, the story was the same. The weather stayed cold, and it snowed again in July and August. There was ice on ponds. People put on their winter clothes and rode in sleighs. No one knew then—and no one really knows now—what made the weather go crazy.

Here's one guess. In April 1815, a giant volcano called Tambora erupted in Indonesia. It filled the atmosphere with tons of ash. Maybe this ash kept out some sunlight for a couple of years and made the Earth colder. However, other huge volcanoes have erupted since Tambora and have not brought on cold spells. The Year Without a Summer is still one of the great weather mysteries.

Into Thin Air — And Back Again

Here's a thought that can make you feel a little dizzy. You — and everything else on Earth — are standing on the outside of a big ball. This ball is whirling through space at over 60,000 miles per hour (over 100,000 km/hr). Not only that, but it's spinning like a top at the same time.

Now here's a thought that's a bit more comforting. As the Earth travels, you're actually inside layers and layers of wrappings. These wrappings keep out a lot of the Sun's burning, harmful rays. They let other rays go through, though, so that the Earth can be warmed. Then, like a soft blanket, they hold the heat in. These layers of wrappings are the Earth's *atmosphere*.

The atmosphere is made of a mixture of gases we call *air*. Air is mostly nitrogen and oxygen, with a little carbon dioxide and other gases. Air also has a lot of dust and water vapor in it. (We'll find out more about these two later in the book.)

Suppose you're returning to Earth from a space mission. You'll hit the first tiny traces of our atmosphere 600 to 300 miles (1000 to 500 km) from Earth. You'll still be in the midnight blackness of the *exosphere*. Then you'll zoom into the *ionosphere*, 300 to 50 miles (500 to 80 km) away from Earth. This is where the mysterious Aurora Borealis appears. (See p.21.)

Next, you will find yourself in the *stratosphere*, 50 to 6 miles (80 to 10 km) from Earth. Now the sky has lightened to a deep violet color. You might see a few very high clouds made of ice crystals. There are swift

Above 300 miles –
EXOSPHERE

320
515

300
483

280
451

260
418

240
386

220
354

200
322

180
290

160
257

140
225

120
193

100
161

80
129

60
96

40
64

20
32

SEA LEVEL

EXOSPHERE
(600 TO 300 MILES)
(1000 TO 500 KM)
FROM EARTH

IONOSPHERE
(300 TO 50 MILES)
(500 TO 80 KM)
FROM EARTH

Aurorae

Meteors
burn up

Noctilucent clouds

Nacreous clouds

Weather
balloons

Concord

STRATOSPHERE
(50 TO 6 MILES)
(80 TO 10 KM)
FROM EARTH

TROPOSPHERE
(6 MILES TO GROUND)
(10 KM TO GROUND)

Mt. Everest

16

winds at the lower edge of the stratosphere, called the *jet stream*. They speed right around the world from west to east. The Concorde supersonic jet flies in the stratosphere. Ordinary jets fly a little lower, but still above most clouds and storms.

When you hit the troposphere, about 6 miles (10 km) from Earth, you're almost home. The sky becomes light blue. There are lots of shifting winds here. Now you can see many clouds, too. Some of them are dropping rain or snow on the ground. The tallest mountains — 3, 4, or 5 miles high (5, 6, or 7 km high) — jut up through the clouds. Their peaks are capped with snow, because high in the troposphere, it's very cold. The air gets warmer as you get closer to the surface of the Earth.

The wrappings of air around the Earth are very heavy. The atmosphere weighs about 6 million billion tons (about 5.5 million billion tonnes). All of this air is pressing on the Earth. Why doesn't it squash you flat? The air isn't just pushing *down* on you. It's pushing in all directions — up, down, and sideways too. Air inside you is pushing out just as hard as air outside you is pushing in.

If you made a stack of all the pillows in your house, you'd see something interesting. The top pillow would stay big and fluffy. But even if the bottom pillow had just as many feathers inside, it would be pressed flat. This means that the feathers in the bottom pillow would be packed together more tightly.

It's the same with the atmosphere. Everything in the world — including the gases in the air — is made of molecules. Molecules are extremely tiny particles that we can see only with the most powerful microscopes. At the "bottom" of the atmosphere, closest to the Earth, the molecules are tightly packed together. This is the right air for us to breathe. The higher in the atmosphere you go, the farther apart the molecules get. Each time you breathe in, you get fewer of the oxygen molecules you need to stay alive. Most climbers who've gone to the top of Mt. Everest, for instance, have used oxygen tanks to breathe. Air at the top of the troposphere — with its molecules widely spread — is lighter than air at the bottom.

We know that the air of the troposphere moves, because that's what wind is: air in motion. In fact, most changes in the weather are caused by air moving. But what makes it move? That's another story.

Amazing Air Tricks

Even though you can't see air, you can prove that it's there by seeing what it does.

I.   I Was Here First!

What you Need:
   a sink
   a plastic drinking glass
   paper towel

What to Do:

1. Fill the sink with water.

2. Push the paper towel into the bottom of the drinking glass. The paper should be wadded up so that it won't fall out when you turn the glass over.

3. Turn the glass upside down. Push the glass straight down into the sink of water, until the water covers the glass. Now lift the glass straight out. Is the paper towel wet or dry?

What's Happening:
Air takes up space, even though we can't see it. The air that was already in the glass kept water from going in and wetting the paper towel.

II.   Weight Right Here

What You Need:
a stick about 1 yard (1 m) long
two balloons the same size
    and shape
string
a pin

What to Do:
1. Blow up the two balloons. Try to make them the same size. Tie off the ends.

2. Use string to tie a balloon to each end of the stick.

3. Tie a string to the midpoint of the stick. Hang the stick somewhere where it won't touch anything. The stick should be balanced so that the two balloons are even with each other.

4. Now use the pin to pop one of the balloons. The heavier balloon dips down right away. Which one is that? What is making it heavier?

Air Force

You can see air pressure at work every time you suck juice out of a bottle.

What You Need:
a bottle of juice
a straw
plasticine

What to Do:
1. Put the straw into the bottle. Suck some juice through the straw. Sluuuurp! No problem, right?

2. Now seal the mouth of the bottle with plasticine. The only opening will be where the straw goes into the bottle.

3. Take another little sip. It's a little more of a challenge now, isn't it?

4. Take off the plasticine. Make a hole about halfway along the straw. (The hole shouldn't be in your mouth when you sip, and it shouldn't be in the juice, either.)

5. Try sucking some juice up the straw with the hole in it. Having any luck?

What's Happening?
When you first sucked on the straw, what you were really doing was taking air out of it. Once you do that, air pressure inside the straw is less than air pressure outside it. Air outside the straw presses down on the surface of the juice, forcing it up the straw. When you cover the mouth of the bottle with plasticine, no more air can get into the bottle. There's less air to push down on the juice and force it up the straw. If you make a hole in the straw, you can't suck all the air out of it so that the juice will come up. Why? More air keeps rushing into the straw through the hole.

Northern Lights

Imagine a huge, shimmering curtain of light across the night sky. As you watch, its shape seems to change. Its colors change, too, from pink to violet to green. In Canada's far north, you can do more than imagine this breath-taking light show. You can step outside and see it. This is the Aurora Borealis, or Northern Lights. What makes the Northern Lights light up? Tiny particles called *electrons* speed to Earth from the Sun. Each electron carries an electrical charge. When the electrons hit the very cold gases of the upper atmosphere, they make the gases glow. Different gases make different colors. For instance, oxygen makes green light, and nitrogen makes pink.

P.S. In a very small way, neon signs work like this too. In these signs, electricity running through a glass tube filled with gas makes colored lights. Different gases are used to make different colors. For example, a gas called *neon* is used for red signs.

Under Pressure

A barometer measures atmospheric pressure — how much the air is pressing down. You can use it to forecast the weather.

What You Need:
a clear plastic bottle
a wide-mouthed jar into which the plastic bottle will fit snugly
ink or food coloring
china marker or any other marker
   that can write on glass
ruler

a rainy day

What to Do:
1. Choose a rainy day — when atmospheric pressure is low — to make this barometer. Otherwise, it won't work for you.

2. Put some water into the bottom of the jar. Add a little ink or food coloring to the water so that it will be easier to see.

3. Turn the bottle upside down and set it in the mouth of the jar, as shown in the drawing.

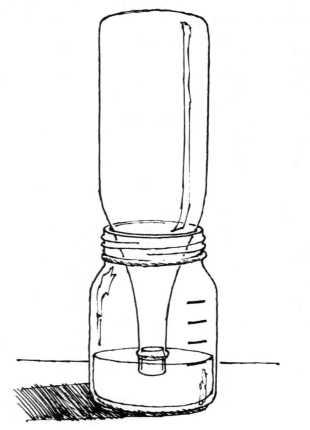

The fit should be snug enough to keep the bottle from touching the bottom of the jar.

4. Is the water rising a little into the neck of the bottle? If not, add a little more water.

5. Let the barometer sit for 15 or 20 minutes. Then check the water level. Make a little line on the side of the jar to show the water level. This is your low pressure mark.

Here's an important tip. The barometer should be at your *eye level* when you make your low pressure mark. If you're looking down at the water (or up at it), you'll put the mark in the wrong place. Don't move the jar, because this will make the water slosh. Just bend your knees (or do whatever you need to do) to get the water even with your eyes. Then do the same thing when you take a reading.

6. Use a ruler to measure ½ inch (1 cm) from the low pressure mark. Make another little line. Do this twice more, so that you have three lines above the first line you made. The lines should be ½ inch (1 cm) apart.

7. Put your barometer on a flat surface where you can check it easily. Look at it every morning and every night. When the water is at the lowest mark, it means wet weather. The two middle marks mean that the weather is changing. The highest mark means fine, dry weather.

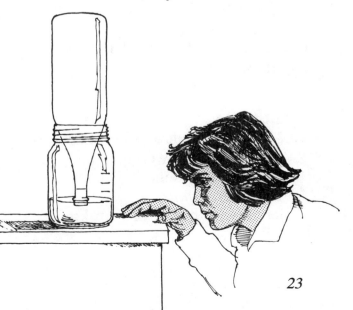

Go Fly a Kite

Find a current of air going upward, and a kite that you made yourself can catch a ride on it.

What You Need:
Two 2 foot (70 cm) pieces of 0.2 inch (5 mm) doweling
a tape measure or measuring stick
a soft lead pencil or grease pencil
40 inches (100 cm) nylon fishing line
scissors
44 yards (40 m) nylon cord
4 thumbtacks
a square at least 3 feet x 3 feet
   (80 cm x 80 cm) cut from a strong
   plastic garbage bag
tape
14 strips of tissue paper, each
   6 inches x 12 inches
   (15 cm x 30 cm)
6 inch (15 cm) flat wooden stick
a curtain ring

What to Do:

1. Measure 8 inches (20 cm) on one piece of doweling. Mark the spot with pencil. This piece will be the *spine* (the lengthwise piece) of your kite.

2. Measure and mark 12 inches (35 cm) on the other piece of doweling. This will be the *spar* (the crossbar) of your kite.

3. Hold the spar against the spine so that the two marks line up. Ask someone to wind the nylon fishing line around and around the two pieces, to hold them together. Tie the line with good, strong knots. This is your kite frame. (See Drawing 1.)

4. Cut a piece of nylon cord 15 feet (4.5 m) long.

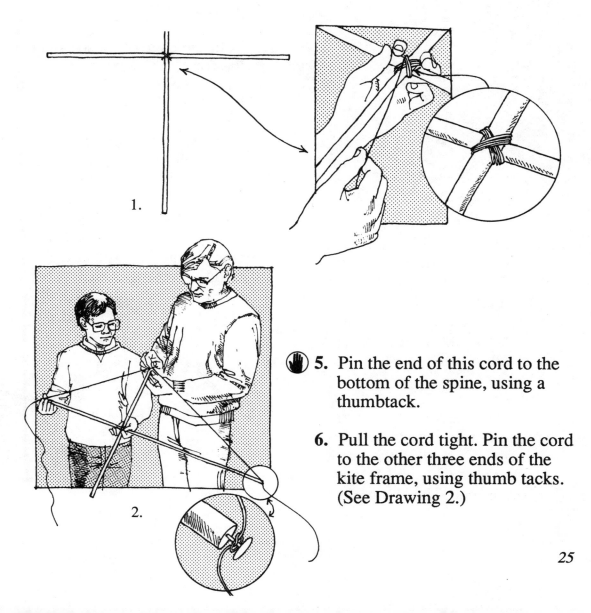

1.

2.

5. Pin the end of this cord to the bottom of the spine, using a thumbtack.

6. Pull the cord tight. Pin the cord to the other three ends of the kite frame, using thumb tacks. (See Drawing 2.)

25

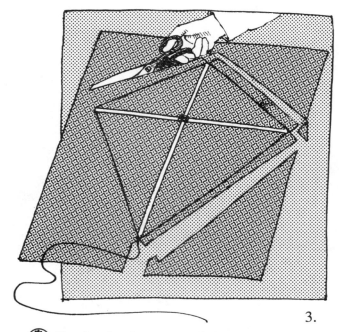

3.

9. Cut little v-shapes out of the plastic to each corner of the kite. (This will let you fold the plastic neatly.)

10. Fold the edge of plastic over the frame and tape it in place. Make sure the plastic is pulled tight and smooth.

11. Cut 4 feet (120 cm) of nylon cord. Fold it in half to make a loop. Push the looped end through the curtain ring. Then pull the loose ends back through the loop. Now the ring should be fixed at the midpoint of the cord.

✋ **7.** At the bottom of the spine, where you started, pull out the first thumbtack. Now push it in again through *two* thicknesses of cord. The piece of cord left over will make your kite tail, so *don't* cut it off.

8. Lay the frame on the garbage bag plastic square. Tape it in a couple of places to hold it while you cut. Cut around the frame, leaving about 1 inch (2 cm) extra all around. (See Drawing 3.)

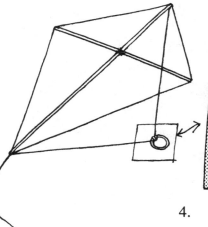
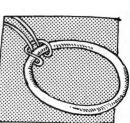

4.

26

12. Tie one end of this cord to the top of the kite and one end to the bottom. This is called the kite *bridle*.

13. Fold the 14 tissue strips in half along their lengths. Fold them in half again to make long, thin strips.

14. Tie the tail of the kite around the middle of each strip. Leave about 6 inches (15 cm) between strips.

15. You still have a piece of nylon cord left, about 37 yards (34 m) long. Tie one end of the cord to the curtain ring. Tie the other end of the cord to the flat stick. Wrap the cord around it. This is the handle for your kite and the cord you need to fly it.

Flying Your Kite
It takes practice to fly a kite well, so don't give up. You may have to make some changes to your kite, too. If it keeps taking nosedives, try making the tail longer. If it falls out of the sky tailfirst, try making the tail shorter. Choose the right day: you need a steady breeze but not a strong, gusting wind. Choose the right place: you need a clear area away from trees and power lines. Ask a friend to toss the kite into the air as you run along with the line.

Why Do We Need the Ozone Layer?

High in the stratosphere is a layer of gas called *ozone*. In 1977, a group of people studying this part of the atmosphere made a startling discovery. They found a hole in the ozone layer over the Antarctic. In the past 10 years, this hole has become bigger. Most people studying the ozone layer think it is being broken down by chemicals called CFCs. They're found in aerosol spray cans and the coolant used in refrigerators. Why should we care if a gas in the stratosphere is disappearing?

The ozone layer shields the Earth from 90 percent of the Sun's ultraviolet (burning) rays. This is very important to us. If people receive too much ultraviolet radiation, they suffer a bad sunburn. Worse, after years of this, they may get skin cancer. Too much ultraviolet radiation will also kill food crops. In September 1987, 40 countries signed a treaty promising to cut the world's output of CFCs in half by 1994. Let's hope this will save our ozone layer — and our skins.

Air on the Move

*L*ong ago, people thought that it was warmer up in the sky — or even on high mountaintops — than down where they lived. After all, they thought, the higher you go, the closer you are to the Sun. They were wrong, though. The higher you go in the troposphere, the colder it gets.

Here's the secret. It's true that the energy we need comes from the Sun. But most of our heat comes from the Earth! The ground *absorbs* (soaks up) the Sun's rays and *re-radiates* them (sends them out again) as heat. The Earth gives most of its heat to the air closest to it.

When air is heated, its molecules begin to move around, faster and faster. They bump into each other and push each other apart. Air with its molecules spread apart is lighter than air with its molecules packed close together. So you would expect warm air to rise — and it does.

Where warm, light air is rising, it isn't pushing so hard against the Earth. We call this a *low pressure* area. Colder, heavier air rushes *toward* low pressure areas to replace the warm air that rose. We call this rushing air *wind*. Where cold, heavy air is slowly sinking to the Earth, it forms a *high pressure* area. Air always moves from a higher pressure area to one with lower pressure. So winds travel *away* from high pressure areas.

The Equator, you remember, is the hottest part of the Earth. As you might expect, warm air rises there, and spreads out. It heads toward the North and South Poles. Before it gets that far, though, it cools down and becomes heavier. It sinks back to Earth and heads back toward the Equator. The winds that rush toward the Equator from north and south are called the trade winds. These winds don't blow straight at the Equator; they blow at an angle. Why?

The Earth is *rotating* (going around) on its axis. To understand what this means, imagine the Earth spinning on a stick that goes from the North Pole to the South Pole. The stick is the Earth's axis. If you have a globe, you can see for yourself what this spinning will do to winds.

Put the index finger of your right hand on the North Pole. Now trace a straight line down to the Equator, without taking your finger off the globe. *At the same time*, give the globe a spin to the right with your other hand. What happens to your finger? It veers off to the side, doesn't it? This is what happens to the winds as they blow over the spinning Earth. It's called the *Coriolis Effect*. In the Northern Hemisphere, the trade winds blow from northeast to southwest. In the Southern Hemisphere, they blow from southeast to northwest.

There are other strong, steady winds that blow nearly all the time. You can see them in the drawing on p.31. There are all kinds of smaller winds, too. They may only blow in one place, or at one time of the year.

Hurricanes are storms with very high winds — up to 200 miles per hour (320 km/hr) — traveling in spirals. They are born in the Atlantic Ocean near the Equator. Then they head northwest toward the West Indies and the coast of the United States. On a satellite picture, hurricanes look like pinwheels. The Coriolis Effect puts a spin on the winds rushing toward the center of the hurricane. Perhaps you can guess what's at the center of a hurricane — a very low pressure area. Hurricanes kill hundreds of people each year.

On a hot summer day, people who live on islands or along a coast can look forward to "sea breezes" blowing in from the sea. During the daytime, land is heated much more quickly by the sun than big bodies of water can be. This means that there's a low pressure area on land. Cooler air blows in from the sea. At night, though, land cools down more quickly than the water does. Now the land becomes cooler than the water, So, at night, "land breezes" blow out to sea.

Monsoon winds are like sea breezes on a huge scale. During the winter, India's land is cooler than the Indian Ocean to the south. A dry land wind blows across India southward to the sea. During the summer, though, India becomes hotter than the ocean. A cool wind blows from the Indian Ocean, northward across India. This is the summer monsoon, and it carries heavy rain with it. After a parched winter, there is enough water for crops to grow. China, the countries of South-East Asia, and some countries in Africa depend on monsoons. In fact, about half the world's people rely on the monsoons to give them enough food to live.

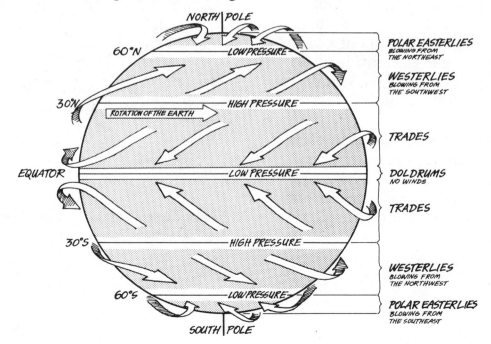

Full of Hot Air

Hot air needs lots of room to rise and spread out — find out for yourself.

I. I Spy-ral

What You Need:
a sheet of heavy paper
pen or pencil
scissors
needle and thread

What to Do:

1. Draw a spiral on a sheet of heavy paper, as shown in the drawing. Cut it out with a pair of scissors. (You cut out a spiral by starting at the outside and going round and round until you reach the center.)

2. Make a hole in the center of the spiral and put a piece of thread through it. (The easiest way to do this is to thread a needle and then pull the needle through the paper.)

3. Knot the thread so it won't pull out of the spiral.

4. Test for rising currents of warm air in your house. Hold the spiral over radiators or light bulbs that have been on for awhile. (Do not hold your spiral over hot stoves, candles, or anything else with a flame.) If there is rising warm air, your spiral will let you know by spinning.

II. Balloon Blow-up

What You Need:
a plastic bottle
a balloon
a bucket

What to Do:
1. Cool the plastic bottle in the refrigerator.

2. Stretch the end of the balloon over the neck of the bottle.

3. Fill the bucket with hot (not boiling) water.

4. Put the bottle and the balloon in the hot water. What happens? Why do you think it happens?

5. Now try putting the bottle and balloon (still joined) back in the refrigerator. What happens? Why?

Blowin' in the Wind

Have you ever seen a windsock — perhaps at a small airport? You can make a windsock that shows the direction the wind is blowing. It also gives you an idea of how strong the wind is.

What You Need:
sleeve of an old, adult-size
   long-sleeve shirt
scissors
16 inches (40 cm) light wire
sewing needle
thread
small stone or other weight
3½ feet (1 m) string

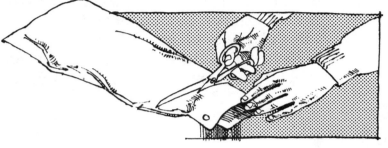

What to Do:

1. Use scissors to cut the shirtsleeve off the shirt. Cut the sleeve in half.

2. Bend the wire into a circle.

3. Fit the wire circle into one end of the sleeve. Fold the edge of the sleeve over the wire and sew it in place with a few stitches. This makes the mouth of the windsock.

4. Wrap the stone in a little bit of the cloth near the wire circle. Take a couple of stitches in the cloth to hold the stone in place.

5. Tie one end of the string to the wire circle, across the opening from the stone.

6. Tie the other end of the string to a clothesline or tree branch. Put the windsock in a place where it can move freely. The stone will keep the mouth of the windsock facing into the wind. How does the windsock look on a very still day? How does it look in a strong wind?

AMAZING FACTS

They Call the Wind Haboob

Willy-Willy sounds cute and harmless, doesn't it? It isn't, though. It's the Australian name for a hurricane. Many winds of the world have colorful names. In the Sudan, the *Haboob* (from the Arabic word for "blowing furiously") is a strong wind that whips up sandstorms. The *Witch's Wind*, also called the Santa Ana, is a hot dry wind in Southern California. This wind can fan brush fires that burn for days. *Chinooks* are warm winds that sweep down the eastern slope of the Rocky Mountains. In the middle of an Alberta winter, a Chinook can suddenly raise the temperature by 36°F (20°C) in a few minutes!

It's a Breeze!

Make yourself an anemometer — an instrument that measures the speed of the wind.

What You Need:
strong thread or fine nylon fishing line—about 12 inches (30 cm) long
glue
a ping-pong ball
a protractor—the biggest one you can find
a friend to help you

What to Do:
1. Glue one end of the line to the ping-pong ball. Glue the other end to the center point on the base of a protractor. This is your anemometer.

2. Hold your anemometer level, with the base of the protractor up. Make sure the ball can swing freely. Hold the anemometer away from your body. You do not want to block the wind.

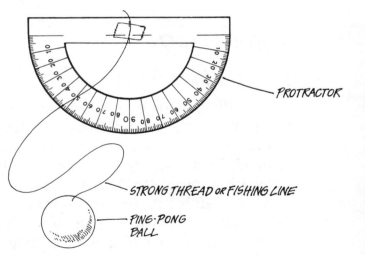

PROTRACTOR

STRONG THREAD or FISHING LINE

PING-PONG BALL

3. When there is no wind at all, the ball should hang straight down. This will be at the 90 degree mark on the protractor.

4. Now hold your anemometer so that it points into the wind. The ping pong ball will swing. Ask a friend to read the angle on the protractor.

The chart below shows you about how strong the wind is:

ANGLE														
90	85	80	75	70	65	60	55	50	45	40	35	30	25	20
MILES PER HOUR														
0	5.8	8.2	10.1	11.8	13.4	14.9	16.4	18.0	19.6	21.4	23.4	25.8	28.7	32.5
KILOMETRES PER HOUR														
0	9.3	13.2	16.3	19.0	21.6	24.0	26.4	29.0	31.5	34.4	37.6	41.5	46.2	52.3

A Low Blow

This air pressure trick surprises just about everyone. And you know what else? If this trick didn't work out the way it's supposed to, airplanes couldn't fly!

What You Need:
2 ping pong balls
2 pieces of string about 6 inches
   (15 cm) long
glue
a stick about 6 inches (15 cm) long

What to Do:
1. Glue one end of a piece of string to a ping pong ball. Repeat with the other string and ping pong ball.

2. Tie the other ends of the strings to the stick, about 2 inches (5 cm) apart.

3. You're going to blow between the two ping pong balls. What do you think will happen when you do? Hold the stick up, quite near your face. Now give it a try. Surprising, isn't it?

What's Happening?
When you blow between the two ping pong balls, you make a low pressure area between them. The air on the outer side of the two balls is higher pressure, so it pushes in. The balls are pushed together.

Why was the little rush of air you made lower pressure than the air around it? The answer is that it was going *faster*. A man named Daniel Bernoulli worked this out over 200 years ago. Airplane wings are designed so that air going over the top of the wing will go faster than air going underneath. This means that there'll be lower pressure above the wing than below it. And *that* means that the higher-pressure air under the wing will push it upward, and keep the plane in the air.

Brrr!

You're hurrying to school on a wintry morning. You rush around the corner and now you're passing a big open field. Suddenly, it feels much colder, as the wind cuts through your jacket and mitts. That's wind chill! Wind chill is a way of measuring how cold the weather will feel to your body.

Here's how to read a wind chill chart. Put one index finger on the temperature — say, 40°F. Put the other index finger on a wind speed — say, 15 miles per hour (mph). Pull the temperature finger down until it's even with the wind finger. Then bring the wind finger across to the temperature finger. The number where your fingers meet is the wind chill temperature. Even if the temperature is only 40°F, this blustery day would feel more like 22°F. You'd have to bundle up warmly before you went outside. Looking at the chart, can you answer this question: Which would feel colder, a day with a temperature of 30°F and a wind speed of 20 miles per hour, or a day with a temperature of 10°F and 5 mile per hour winds?

Wind Chill Temperature

Temperature °C								
Wind Speed (km/h)	0	-5	-10	-15	-20	-25	-30	-35
10	-2	-7	-12	-17	-22	-27	-32	-38
20	-7	-13	-19	-25	-31	-37	-43	-50
30	-11	-17	-24	-31	-37	-44	-50	-57
40	-13	-20	-27	-34	-41	-48	-55	-62
50	-15	-22	-29	-36	-44	-51	-58	-66
60	-16	-23	-31	-38	-45	-53	-60	-68

Temperature °F								
Wind Speed (mph)	40	30	20	10	0	-10	-20	-30
5	37	28	16	6	-5	-15	-26	-36
10	28	16	4	-9	-21	-33	-46	-58
15	22	9	-5	-18	-36	-45	-58	-72
20	18	4	-10	-25	-39	-53	-67	-82
25	16	0	-15	-29	-44	-59	-74	-88
30	13	-2	-18	-33	-48	-63	-79	-94
35	11	4	-20	-35	-49	-67	-82	-98

The Great Water Cycle

Did you ever go outside on a morning so cold that you could see your breath? Did you ever pour a glass of lemonade on a hot day and watch water trickle down the glass? Did you ever see a puddle of water drying up in the sun? In a mystery story called "The Search for the Great Water Cycle," these things might be some of the clues.

Earth is a watery planet. About three-quarters of the Earth is covered by oceans, seas, lakes, bays, and rivers. There's also frozen water in the polar ice-caps and in glaciers. (*Glaciers* are ancient sheets of ice high in the mountains.) A little of Earth's water is also in the atmosphere, in the form of a gas.

For at least 3 billion years, Earth has been using the same water, over and over and over. The rain that falls in your backyard has fallen to Earth countless times before. This means that rainwater must have a way to get back up to the sky so that it can come down again. Yet we never see raindrops traveling up! What's happening?

When water is heated, its molecules begin to bounce around more rapidly. You can see this happening when you boil water on the stove. (But never use the stove without permission, please!) The water rolls and bubbles as the molecules become more active. Some of them leap right into the air and become a gas called *water vapor*. When water turns into a gas, we say that it *evaporates*. Because we can't see or even smell water vapor, we think the water has disappeared. It's still there, though, in the air around us.

When the Sun shines on a puddle, it "dries up." Now you know what's really happening. The heat of the Sun turns the water into water vapor. Most of the water vapor in our atmosphere comes from the oceans. The sun shines on them, and a little of their water evaporates. Some water vapor in the air comes from living things. Plants, for instance, breathe out, or *transpire*, huge amounts of water vapor.

The warmer the air is, the more water vapor it can hold. Do you remember what happens to warm air? It rises, and it carries the water vapor up with it. When warm air rises, though, it gets colder. (Remember, too, that air gets colder the higher you go in the troposphere.) Cold air can't hold as much water vapor as warm air, so some of the water vapor turns back into water droplets. This is called *condensation*. It's the first step toward making clouds, rain, and snow.

You've probably made water vapor condense into water lots of times. On a hot summer day, a glass of cold lemonade can cool the air around it. This air can't hold all its water vapor any more. Some of it condenses on the outside of the glass. Every time you breathe out, you put a little water vapor into the air. If the air is very cold, the water vapor condenses into little water droplets. You see them as a white mist in front of your face.

Dew looks like diamonds glittering on spider webs and blades of grass. You have to get up early to see it, because the sun will soon dry it up. If a hot day is followed by a chilly night, the ground will cool down quickly. The air just above the ground will be chilled, too. Then it won't be able to hold all the water vapor it collected during the day. So droplets of dew form by condensation. People often talk about dew "falling," but it doesn't really fall from anywhere. It was right there in the air all along.

Now do you see why I called the great water cycle a mystery story? A lot of it is hidden from us, even though it's happening right before our eyes. You'll probably be happy to move along to the parts of the water cycle we *can* see — clouds, rain, and snow.

The Fog Harps of Atacama

In the Atacama Desert in Chile people sometimes make fog harps. These look a bit like musical harps, but no songs are ever played on them. The Atacama Desert has almost no rainfall. It does have fog, though, which blows in from the Pacific Ocean. The fog droplets hit the tightly stretched nylon strings of the harps. In just one day, almost 3 gallons (more than 10 L) of water can be collected on 11 square feet (1 square meter) of strings.

Now You See It; Now You Don't

Find out for yourself what things help water to evaporate more quickly.

What You Need:
2 saucers
paper towels
a small plate
a small bottle
measuring spoons

What to Do:

1. Measure 2 tablespoons (30 mL) of water into each saucer. Put one in direct sunlight. Put the other saucer in the shade. Which saucer of water evaporates first? Why do you think it happens this way?

2. Drop 1 tablespoon (15 mL) of water in the center of a paper towel square. Repeat this on another square. Leave one square to dry on the counter. Flap the other square to make a breeze or take it into a real breeze outside. Which square dries faster?

3. Put 2 tablespoons (30 mL) of water on a plate. Put another 2 tablespoons (30 mL) of water in a small bottle. Put them side by side and check them after a couple of hours. Which water evaporates more quickly — the water that is spread out flat on the plate, or the water in the bottle? Why do you think it happens this way?

Pure and Simple

If the Earth's water just keeps going around and around, how come it doesn't get dirtier and dirtier? The secret is *distillation*.

What You Need:
a large plastic dishpan
a ruler
a drinking glass (it has to be
    shorter than the sides of
    the dishpan)
a small wooden block
clear plastic food wrap
masking tape

a hot, sunny day

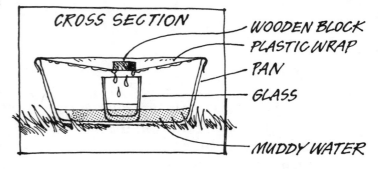

CROSS SECTION — WOODEN BLOCK — PLASTIC WRAP — PAN — GLASS — MUDDY WATER

What to Do:
1. Put 2 inches (5 cm) of clean tap water into the dishpan. (Measure with the ruler.) Now add a little garden dirt to make the water look muddy.

2. Set the glass upright in the middle of the dishpan. If it's a light-weight glass that won't stay put, find a heavier glass.

3. Cover the pan with plastic wrap and stretch it tight and smooth. If it isn't the kind that sticks to itself, tape it with masking tape. (This is a lot easier for two people, one to stretch and one to tape.)

4. Put the wooden block on the center of the plastic wrap, right over where the glass is. This is to make the plastic sag a little toward the center. However, it is important that the block isn't *resting on* the glass.

5. Put the dishpan where the sun can shine on it all day. Later in the day, check the pan. You'll see that water drops will form inside the plastic wrap. They'll drip into the glass. At the end of the day, take a look at the water in the glass. Are you surprised?

What's Happening?

As the water heats and evaporates (turns into water), the bits of dirt are left in the bottom of the pan. When the water vapor rises to the cooler plastic wrap, it condenses again. The water drops roll downward to the center of the wrap and drip into the glass. The water in the glass has been cleaned of most impurities. This way of purifying water is called *distillation*.

Unfortunately, some of the harmful chemicals we put into the air can't be cleaned out of the water supply in this way. For example, factory chimneys may put sulfur dioxide into the air. This gas changes into bits of sulfate in the air. When water droplets condense on bits of sulfate, they fall to Earth as *acid rain*. Acid rain may be carried by wind and clouds to fall hundreds of kilometers away from where the pollution started. Acid rain can poison lakes, damage buildings, and kill trees.

It's Hair-raising!

Human hairs stretch or shorten, depending on how hot and humid the weather is. You can use a human hair to make a hygrometer, which measures how much water is in the air.

What You Need:

a straight human hair, at least 10 inches (25 cm) long
detergent
a 1 quart (1 L) milk carton
art knife (available in art and stationery stores)
a paper clip
a darning needle with a big eye
sticky tape
a penny
a toothpick
a small sheet of paper

1.

SLIDE IN THE
PAPER CLIP

AFTER CUTTING
THE "H" FOLD UP
THE PANELS AS
SHOWN ABOVE

What to Do:

1. Wash the milk carton with water and detergent. (Otherwise, sour milk will make the carton smell *awful*.) Let the carton dry.

2. Ask an adult to do this part for you. With the art knife, cut a slit in the carton, about 1 inch (3 cm) from the spout end.

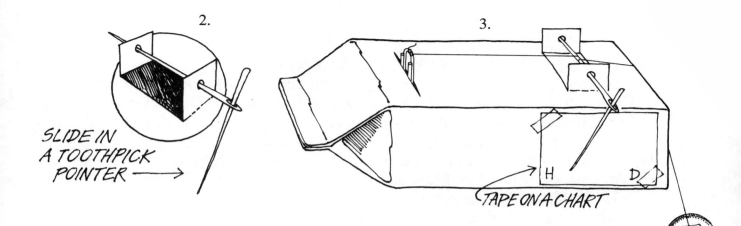

2.

SLIDE IN
A TOOTHPICK
POINTER ──→

3.

TAPE ON A CHART

H   D

3. Push the paper clip halfway into the slit in the carton.

4. With the knife, carefully make three cuts in the carton to form an H. The cuts should be about 1 inch (3 cm) from the flat end of the carton, on the same side as the paperclip slit. Fold the two flaps you make so that they're sticking *out* from the carton. (See Drawing 1.)

5. Push the darning needle through the two flaps. Twist the needle around a few times. The holes should be big enough that the needle can spin easily. (See Drawing 2.)

6. Push a toothpick through the eye of the needle to make a pointer. (See Drawing 2.) Make sure the toothpick is not touching the side of the carton.

7. Tie one end of the hair to the paper clip. Wrap the hair once around the needle. (See Drawing 3.)

8. Tape the penny to the end of the hair. Now let the penny hang down at the end of the carton. (See Drawing 3.)

9. Tape a piece of paper to the side of the carton, under the pointer. (See Drawing 3.)

ake your hygrometer into the bathroom after someone has had a shower and it's still hot and steamy. Watch as the hair stretches and the pointer moves. Wait until the pointer stops moving. Mark an H (for humid) on the paper where the toothpick is pointing. Mark a D (for dry) on the other side of the paper.

11. Set your hygrometer on a table or shelf and watch it from day to day. You will see the pointer move a little toward H when it rains, and a little toward D when it is very dry.

What's Humidity?

Warm air can hold more water vapor than cold air. The amount of water vapor in the air is called the *absolute humidity*. People are usually more interested in the *relative humidity*. This is the amount of water vapor in the air compared with the greatest amount it could possibly hold at that temperature. When the relative humidity is 90 percent on a hot summer day, we feel very sticky and uncomfortable. Do you know why? The air is already holding nearly all the water it can. This means that the sweat on our skin can't evaporate to cool us off.

4.

Dew Drop In

Ever wonder how much dew condenses in your yard? Here's an easy way to find out.

What You Need:
a spade
a piece of plastic (a garbage
   bag is good)
four heavy stones
a jar with a tight-fitting lid

What to Do:
1. Dig a hole in the ground about 2 to 3 inches (5 to 8 cm) deep. (Ask permission *before* you dig!)

2. Before the sun goes down, line the hole with plastic. Push the plastic down into the hole so that it makes a little bowl. Put stones around the hole to hold the plastic in place.

It's best to start your dew collecting on a clear night. A night when the weather forecast says the temperature will drop 18°F (10°C) or more would be best. Maybe you can telephone your local weather office and ask whether dew is expected tonight.

3. Early the next morning, go out and collect your dew. Carefully lift the plastic out and pour the dew into the jar. Put the lid onto the jar.

4. If you have good weather, you can collect dew for a week or so. (Rain doesn't count — don't add it to your jar.) Keep the lid on the jar so that the dew doesn't evaporate. Are you surprised at how much dew you collected?

Dew collects more on things that cool down quickly, such as blades of grass, than on things that hold heat, such as black paving stones. Notice which things in your yard collect the heaviest covering of dew. You'll know that these are the things that became coolest overnight.

Kinds of Weather

Clouds Up Close

People sometimes describe clouds as "castles in the air" or "featherbeds in the sky." Some clouds look so soft and fluffy that it's easy to imagine snuggling down in them. Do you know what it would really be like to wrap yourself in a cloud?

Have you ever been outside when it's foggy? The dampness seems to cut right through your clothes. The houses on your street disappear into gray mist. That's what a cloud is really like. In fact, fog is just a cloud that's close to the ground.

If you could look up the recipe for a cloud in a cookbook, here's what it would say:

1. Start with some water.
2. Heat the water until it turns into water vapor and rises in the air.
3. Wait until the rising air cools.
4. Stir in some dust or salt or tiny bits of ice.
5. Water vapor will condense to form droplets.

You know about steps 1 to 3 already (if you've read pages 40 to 42). Step 4 may be a surprise. To make a cloud, you need something for the water droplets to cling to. A cloud is a gathering of billions of tiny water droplets. Each water droplet condenses on a bit of dust, or salt from a sea-breeze. (If the cloud forms high in the troposphere, where it is very cold, water vapor will change into ice crystals instead of water droplets.)

Although there are a few clouds in the stratosphere — probably made of ice crystals — nearly all clouds form in the troposphere. There are three main kinds of clouds. *Cirrus* clouds look like little wisps of hair or feathers. Their name comes from the Latin for "curl of hair." *Cumulus* clouds look like a pile of cotton puffs. Their name comes from the Latin for "heap." *Stratus* clouds are sheets of cloud across the sky. Their name comes from the Latin for "spread out."

Wispy cirrus clouds are by far the highest clouds. They float 16,500 to 45,000 feet (5000 to 14,000 m) above the ground. They're made of tiny ice crystals. Sometimes cirrus clouds join together to form a silky-looking veil. When the sun or the moon shines through these clouds, the ice veil makes a halo around them.

Cumulus clouds are usually between 1000 and 15,000 feet (300 and 5000 m) above the ground. When they float lazily through a blue sky in a small or medium-sized puffs, they're fair weather clouds. When they look bigger, and darker, rain or snow is probably on the way. One kind of cumulus cloud, the *cumulonimbus*, brings thunderstorms.

Cumulonimbus clouds form huge towers in the sky. These clouds can billow up to a height of 9 miles (15 km) in just an hour. Their tops are flat and jut out in the direction the storm is moving. Their bases are dark gray. Inside cumulonimbus clouds, there are fierce winds blowing upward and sweeping down again. Pilots are careful to avoid these big violent clouds, which can give even a jumbo jet a very rough ride.

Stratus clouds are the lowest clouds. They can be anywhere from 1500 feet (500 m) in the air right down to ground level. They form a dreary gray sheet across the sky, blocking out the sun. Stratus clouds often bring a light, steady rain or fine grains of snow. When stratus clouds form at ground level, we call them *fog*.

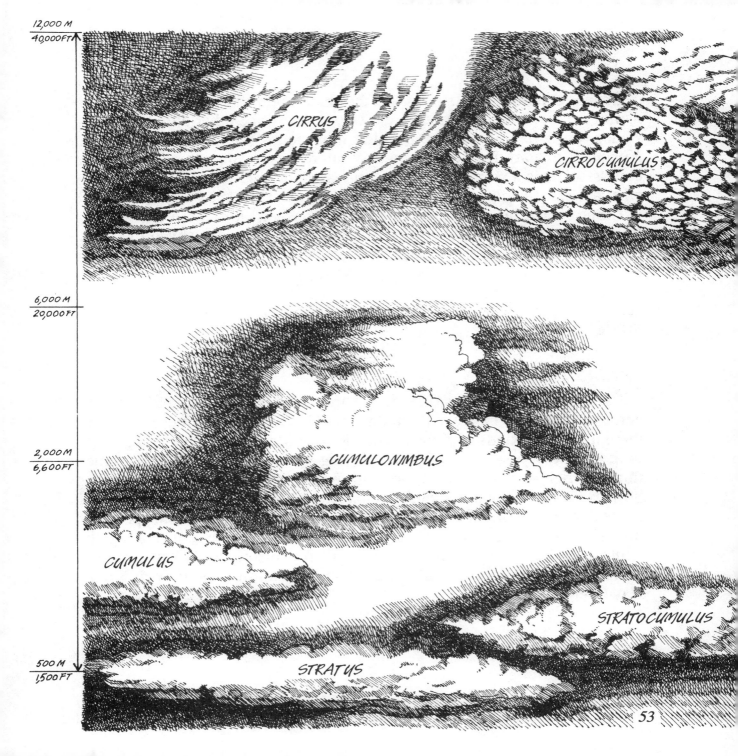

12,000 M
40,000FT

CIRRUS

CIRROCUMULUS

6,000 M
20,000FT

CUMULONIMBUS

2,000 M
6,600FT

CUMULUS

STRATOCUMULUS

500 M
1,500FT

STRATUS

53

Cirrus, cumulus, and stratus are the three main kinds of clouds. Their names can be combined in different ways to describe other clouds. For instance, *cirrocumulus* clouds are high thin clouds with a rippled pattern. *Nimbus* is a word that's added on to cloud names to show that they're rain clouds. *Altus* is a word added to show that clouds are high. Can you guess what a *nimbostratus* cloud would look like? What about an *altostratus*?

Clouds trace fascinating, ever-changing designs across the sky. Sometimes there are two or three different kinds of clouds in the sky at the same time. How many different clouds have you seen?

SOMETHING TO DO

Sky Stories

All you need to tell sky stories is a warm day with a few clouds drifting across a blue sky. (I always think that cumulus clouds have more stories in them than other kinds of clouds.) Just lie back somewhere comfortable and look up. Do you see fluffy kittens playing with a ball of wool? Or something scarier — maybe a dragon, with puffs of smoke coming out of her nostrils? As you watch a cloud, its shape slowly changes. Maybe you can make a story out of that. Perhaps the dragon was under a wicked spell, but now she's returning to her real shape — a fearless princess, riding a great white horse! Its fun to tell a cloud story to someone else. You can take turns. Two people's stories about the same cloud might be very different. Have fun!

Cloud in a Bottle

It sounds crazy, but it's true — with a bottle and a bicycle pump, you can make your own little cloud.

What You Need:

a pump
a 1 gallon (4 L) clear bottle or jug — the kind cider comes in is just right
a cap for the bottle
a measuring cup
a partner

What to Do:

1. Pour about ½ cup (125 mL) of water into the bottle. Holding your hand over the mouth of the bottle, give it a shake to wet the sides of the bottle.

2. Ask an adult to punch a hole in the bottle's cap for you. The hole should be about ¼ inch (0.5 cm) across.

3. Place the cap on the bottle, upside down. (Why upside down? So that, when you need to, you can lift it away from the bottle very quickly.)

4. Hold the end of the pump hose tightly against the cap on the bottle.

5. While you're holding tight, ask your partner to make two or three strokes on the pump. (Not more!)

6. Quickly pull the cap away. You'll hear a popping sound, and you'll see a cloud in the bottle.

What's Happening?
The air inside the bottle is pushed together by the pump. This makes the air warm up. Some of the water in the jug turns into water vapor. (Did you remember that warm air can hold more water vapor than cool air?) Then, when you snatch off the cap, the air expands (spreads out). It gets cooler and can't hold as much water vapor. So the water vapor condenses into water droplets, making a cloud.

AMAZING FACTS

Trapped in a Thundercloud

U.S. Marine pilot William Rankin had the adventure of his life in 1959. His plane went out of control during a bad storm. He had to bail out at 47,000 feet (14,000 m) with a parachute. Rankin hoped to float gently to earth. Instead he found himself right in the middle of a big, black storm cloud. The winds inside the cloud swept him up, dropped him with a stomach-churning lurch, and bounced him from side to side. Rain and hailstones pelted him. The flashes of lightning were so bright that he had to squeeze his eyes shut. The thunder was a deep rumble that made his whole body shake. Finally, the storm began to die down and Rankin finished his trip to Earth. His terrifying ride through the thundercloud took 40 minutes. It left him with just a few bruises and an amazing story to tell.

What's a Nephoscope?

Which way is the wind blowing, way up where the clouds are? A nephoscope will tell you.

What You Need:

a compass
a mirror small enough to be carried outside
scissors
a sheet of heavy paper
a round dish or jar lid (to use to draw a circle)
a pen

a day with some light clouds passing over

What to Do:

1. Draw a circle in the middle of the paper. (Use a dish or jar lid for a guide.) Make a circle that is a little bit smaller than your mirror.

2. Cut the circle out of the paper so that it has a round hole in the middle.

3. Around the hole in the paper, mark the compass points: N for north, S for south, W for west, and E for east. If you want to be fancy, you can also mark the intermediate (in-between) points. (Look at Drawing 1 for help.)

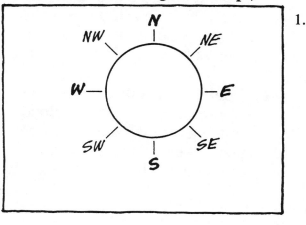

1.

4. Place your mirror under the paper so that the hole is filled in. This is your nephoscope — a thing that lets you check which direction the clouds are moving.

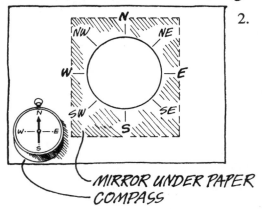

2.

MIRROR UNDER PAPER
COMPASS

5. Take the compass and nephoscope outside. Hold the compass in your hand and turn around until the needle is pointing to N for north. Put your nephoscope on flat ground so that its N is also pointing north.

6. Look down at the mirror. You can see the reflection of clouds floating through the sky. Suppose a cloud first begins to cross the nephoscope at letter E.

This means that, up where the cloud is, the wind is blowing from the east. It is carrying the cloud westward. The cloud will leave the nephoscope at W.

If a cloud starts to cross the mirror at N, where do you think it will leave the mirror? Which way is the wind blowing?

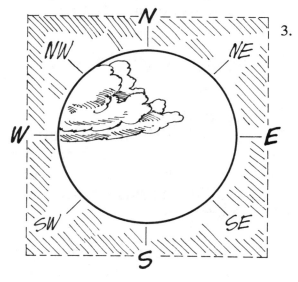

3.

If you made the windsock on p.34, you can check the wind direction down where you are. Is it blowing the same way as it is up where the clouds are?

Terrifying Tornadoes

A tornado is a violent, twisting column of air. It can be seen as a dark, funnel-shaped cloud, wide at the top and narrow at the bottom. This funnel hangs down from a storm cloud. Tornadoes only do damage when the bottom of the funnel touches the ground. If they touch down where people live, they can wreck houses and toss cars — sometimes even trains — right into the air.

- Tornadoes have the fastest winds on Earth — perhaps up to 250 miles per hour (400 km/hr).
- Most tornadoes only touch down for about 10 to 15 minutes.
- Tornadoes usually travel about 6 miles (10 km) before disappearing.
- The path of the usual tornado is only about 140 yards (130 m) wide.
- Tornadoes make a deafening roar as they come close, like a jet plane taking off.

- The United States has more tornadoes than any other country — about 700 a year. Most are in "Tornado Alley" running up the middle of the U.S. Canada has about 50 tornadoes a year. They are most common in southern Manitoba and Ontario, at the end of "Tornado Alley."

Tornadoes are truly terrifying. Remember, though, that even in North America, nearly everybody goes through life without ever seeing a tornado, much less being hurt by one.

AMAZING FACTS

Look Out for Brocken Specters

Long ago, a climber was struggling up the Brocken Mountain in Germany. The weather was wet and gloomy, and he was alone. Suddenly, he saw a gigantic figure looming out of the mist. According to the old story, he was so frightened that he stepped back and fell off the mountain. What did he really see? It was his own shadow. Brocken specters — named for this story — are shadows cast on fog. If you stand on high ground, with your back to the sun, and look down into a fog-filled valley, you may see a Brocken specter. It may be huge: specters up to 200 feet (60 m) long have been reported. You may see a halo of light — called a glory — around the head of your Brocken specter. Here's something strange, though. If a row of people stand looking down at their Brocken specters, they can all see each other's shadows. However, each person can only see his or her own glory!

Rain Check

You can probably think of times when rain spoiled your plans. Maybe your baseball game or your trip to the beach had to be called off. When television weather forecasters have to tell us that rain is coming, they often pull long faces and treat it as sad news.

Even while you're complaining about the rain, though, you probably have a pretty good idea why we need it. Without rain, plants would die, and then people and animals wouldn't have enough to eat. One of the nice things about growing your own garden is that, on rainy days, you can say, "Well, at least it's good for the green beans!"

You may have grandparents who can remember how much Americans and Canadians suffered in the 1930s. In those years, the central part of the United States and the southern Prairies of Canada didn't get enough rain. The land became a "Dust Bowl": the topsoil blew away and crops couldn't grow.

You already know something about how clouds are made. You can't have rain without clouds, but you can often have clouds without rain. What makes a cloud drop some of its water on the Earth? Here's one way it can happen.

Clouds are made of billions of tiny water droplets. Each of these droplets has condensed on a bit of dust. These dust particles are so tiny that you can't see them. The tiny droplets slowly grow larger as more water vapor condenses. The bigger, heavier water droplets begin to sink down through a cloud. As they go, they bump into other water droplets.

The water droplets join together to make bigger and bigger drops. (You've probably seen water drops doing this on windows or the bathroom mirror.) When the water drops become too big and heavy for the cloud to hold them, they fall to the ground.

Raindrops are about 0.04 to 0.2 inches (1 to 5 mm) across. Small as that is, it's about 100 times bigger than the water droplets in a cloud. Most people think of raindrops as teardrop-shaped — pointed at the top and rounded at the bottom. In fact, falling raindrops are rounded on the top and flattened on the bottom — more like the shape of hamburger buns!

Remember those tall, fierce storm clouds, cumulonimbus? These clouds have such strong updrafts (winds going up) that they can keep the raindrops up until they're very large. These raindrops finally come down in a drenching downpour, hitting the pavement so hard that they bounce right up again. Other clouds make smaller raindrops that fall more gently.

Cumulonimbus clouds are the only ones that can make hail. Hailstones are lumps of ice that start out as ordinary raindrops. Then raindrops are swept high in the cloud, so high that they freeze into ice. Other winds inside the cloud carry the ice pieces downward again. Water droplets coat their outsides. Up they go again, and another layer freezes. The longer the hailstones stay in the cloud, bouncing up and down, the bigger they get. Hailstones may be as small as mothballs or as big as baseballs. The larger ones can hurt animals and people. Even the smaller ones can break windows and flatten farmers' fields. It's best to take shelter during a hailstorm. Afterwards, though, you might like to collect a hailstone and cut it open. You can see all the layers of ice inside, like the layers of an onion.

People who study clouds have tried for many years to make rain. (They've also worked on stopping hail.) Sometimes clouds are "seeded," which means that airplanes drop dry ice or other crystals into them. The idea is to make lots of ice crystals form by giving them something to cling to. As they fall to earth, they melt into rain. Often seeded clouds do rain. It's hard to judge how well seeding really works, though. No one can prove the clouds wouldn't have rained anyway, all by themselves.

In the late 1960s scientists of the Soviet Union reported a way of stopping large hailstones. They used rockets to fire chemicals into clouds, so that many tiny hailstones would form, instead of a few big ones. When Western European and North American scientists tried this, they couldn't get it to work as well. The truth is, our efforts to change the weather are still at a very early stage. There'll still be plenty left for you to discover when you're grown up!

The Rainmaker

You don't have to make a trip to the clouds to learn something about how raindrops are made.

What You Need:
kettle
small saucepan
oven mitt
ice cubes

What to Do:

1. Before starting, be sure to ask if it's OK to use the kettle. If not, ask a grownup to make rain with you.

2. Fill the kettle with water. Then heat the kettle and wait until the water boils. When it boils, you can hear bubbling sounds inside, and steam comes out the spout. This steam is very hot and can burn you. Be *very careful* not to put your hands or face over the spout.

3. Put some ice cubes into the saucepan. Cover your hand with an oven mitt. Hold the saucepan by its handle so that the flat bottom of the pot is over the steam. What happens on the underside of the pot?

What's Happening?
When water is heated, it *evaporates*. But when the water vapor touches the cold pot, it *condenses*. The water drops run together to form bigger drops. Finally, they are too big and heavy to cling to the pot, and they fall. This is something like what happens inside a cloud. The water droplets join together until they're so heavy that the cloud can't hold them. Then we have rain.

Raindrop Splatter Art

Sometimes we feel as if the rain has spoiled all our plans. But here's something you can *only* do on a rainy day!

What You Need:
poster paint
paintbrush
white drawing paper

What to Do:

1. Paint some shapes on a piece of drawing paper. Big, bright shapes that are completely colored in will work best. Wait for the paint to dry.

2. Hold your painting out in the rain for just a minute. Hold the paper with both hands and keep it flat so that the paint won't run.

3. Bring the painting inside. Put it somewhere to dry. What kind of pattern have the raindrops made?

AMAZING FACTS

Rainfall Records

The rainiest place in Canada is my home province, British Columbia. Every year, about 260 inches (6655 mm) of rain fall on Henderson Lake. In one especially soggy year, 1931, 319.8 inches (8122.4 mm) fell. The rainiest place in the world, though, is Tutenendo, Colombia. It gets about 460 inches (about 11,770 mm) of rain a year. The driest place in the world is probably the Atacama Desert of Chile. Over a 50 year period, it received only 0.02 inches (0.7 mm) of rain.

A Drop in the Bucket

You *can* catch rain in a bucket — but if you'd like a better idea of how much rain fell, here's how to do it.

What You Need:
a wide-bottomed bottle or jar (Jar W)
a funnel that fits into the bottle — funnel opening should have same
    diameter as bottom of Jar W
a tall narrow straight-sided glass jar
    like the kind olives come in (Jar N)
masking tape
a pen
a ruler
a spade

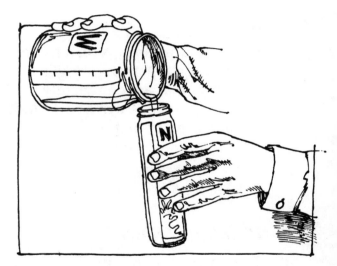

What to Do:
1. Mark a strip of masking tape in half inches or centimeters. Mark 4 inches (10 cm) in all. Stick the masking tape to the side of Jar W. The lowest measurement should be ½ inch (1 cm) from the bottom of the jar. The wide-bottomed jar (Jar W) is your rain gauge.

2. Now pour tap water into the rain gauge until it reaches the

½ inch mark (1 cm mark.) Carefully pour this water into the tall narrow jar (Jar N). Put a piece of masking tape on Jar N. Mark ½ inch (1 cm) at the height the water reaches.

3. Keep measuring water in the rain gauge (Jar W) and pouring it into Jar N until you've got 4 inches (10 cm) marked off on the narrow jar. Why go to all this trouble, you ask? It is much easier for you to read measurements from the tall narrow jar (Jar N), where the lines are farther apart.

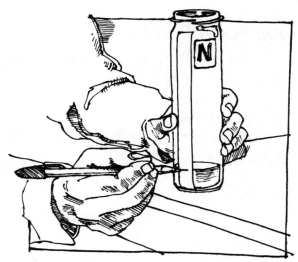

4. Put your rain gauge (Jar W) outside, on flat ground. Choose a place that is clear of bushes, trees, or overhanging roofs.

5. Put the funnel into the mouth of the rain gauge (Jar W). It has to fit in with no gaps. Every morning, pour the rain collected in the last 24 hours into Jar N. Write down the measurement. How much rainfall is your neighborhood getting?

Backyard Rainbow

All you need is a sunny day, a sudden shower (from a garden hose)—and you can see a rainbow!

What You Need:
a garden hose with a fine spray nozzle
a partner to work with

a sunny day

What to Do:

1. Wait until the sun is low in the sky.

2. Turn the hose on. Ask your partner to hold the nozzle up high and pointed downwards to make a fine spray.

3. Stand with your back to the sun. Try to face something dark-colored, such as a large shrub. (This will make your rainbow easier to see.) Look right into the water spray and you should see a small rainbow. (The person holding the hose may not see it, so take turns.)

What's Happening?
To see a rainbow, you need to look into falling rain with the Sun behind you. Sunlight, which you usually see as white light, really has all the colors of the rainbow in it. When the sunlight hits the raindrops, it is bent and split into all its separate colors so that you can see them.

AMAZING FACTS

Raining Cats and Dogs — and Frogs

Did you ever hear people exclaim, "It's raining cats and dogs!" They don't really mean that a shower of furry critters is coming down from the sky. They just mean that it's raining hard. Every once in awhile, though, it seems that animals do fall out of the sky in a rainstorm. Most reports tell of mysterious fish falls. In Trowbridge, England, in 1939, hundreds of small frogs fell from the sky. As they hit the ground, they began to hop around. In Acapulco, Mexico, in 1968, yachts gathered for a race were showered with maggots. Where do these things come from? Probably they are swept up into the clouds by strong, swirling winds, and then dropped with the rain. No one is really sure about this, since no one has seen them go up. People have only seen them come down.

Snow Wonder

People often say that no two snowflakes are alike. You might wonder how we could possibly know this for sure. An American nicknamed "Snowflake" Bentley spent 50 years of his life studying snowflakes. He photographed 6,000 of them and looked at thousands more. All of them were at least a little different from each other. Still, a university professor in Boston, Massachusetts calculated that just one big snowstorm could drop 50 *quadrillion* snowflakes on his city. (That's 5 followed by 16 zeros).

Even if you looked at snowflakes night and day for your whole life, you could never see more than a tiny, tiny fraction of them. Let's say, then, that it's a *good guess* that you will never see two snowflakes that are the same. We can say this because we know something about how snowflakes are made.

Snowflakes are made of two or more *crystals*. Crystals are solids whose molecules are arranged in regular patterns, instead of being stuck together in shapeless blobs. How do snow crystals form?

Snow crystals, like raindrops, are born in clouds. Snow crystals can only form in clouds that are colder than 32°F (0°C). That's the freezing temperature of water. Snow crystals, like raindrops, start with a water droplet condensing on a bit of dust. The water droplet freezes into a tiny ice particle. Then a very interesting thing happens.

There is water vapor — water in the form of gas — in the cloud. Molecules from the water vapor start to stick to the tiny bit of ice. They arrange themselves in neat patterns all around the ice, freezing as they go. Slowly they build up the design of the snow crystal. Because of the way water molecules fit together, most snow crystals are *hexagonal*, which means six-sided. Each snow crystal is made up of about 10^{18} water molecules. (This is the mathematician's tidy way of writing 10 followed by 18 zeros.) This is a huge number of bits to arrange into snow crystal designs.

If someone asked you to picture a snowflake, you'd probably think of a flat, six-pointed star shape. There are lots of different kinds of snow crystals, though. The ones that fall from high, very cold cirrus clouds are six-sided columns. Some of these columns have flat "caps" on the ends, which makes them look like little spools.

If a cloud doesn't have much water vapor, its snow crystals will be small and simple in shape. If the cloud has a lot of water vapor, snow crystals can grow bigger. Lower, warmer clouds — just below the freezing point — usually have more water vapor than higher, colder clouds. At temperatures around 5°F (-15°C) the largest, prettiest crystals are formed — *hexagonal plates* and *stellar* (star-shaped) *crystals.*

These flat, delicate crystals look magically beautiful while they're spinning down out of the sky. No wonder they're many people's favorite. Even the person who shovels snow at your house may like them. This kind of snow makes a light fluffy layer on the ground.

What is your least favorite kind of snow? Many people would choose *needles.* They're thin, pointed snow crystals that sting when they blow against your cheeks. *Graupel* — which are tiny, window-rattling snowballs — aren't much fun for faces either. They're made in an interesting way. They start as small snow crystals formed high in a cloud. Then they fall down into warmer parts of the cloud. There water drops freeze on them. With their new coating — called rime — they finish their trip to Earth.

Take a quick guess. Where do you think the most snow falls: in the Arctic Circle or near the Canadian-American border? The answer may surprise you. The air around the North Pole (and the South Pole, too) is so cold that it doesn't have much water vapor in it. So the snowfalls are light. Ottawa, for instance, has five times as much snow as Alert, in the Northwest Territories.

The snowiest part of the world is from about latitude 66° to latitude 40°. In the Northern Hemisphere, all of the Canadian provinces, the southern parts of the Northwest Territories and the Yukon, and about half of the United States are within these bounds. Farther south, it may snow every once in a while, and there will be snow on high mountains. In fact, Mount Kenya, which has snow on its peak, is right on the Equator!

AMAZING FACTS

What's a Snowroller?

A snowroller looks as if somebody started to roll a ball of snow for a snowman, and then punched a hole right in the middle. It also looks a bit like a big sugar doughnut. Snowrollers aren't made by people, though. They're made by the wind in big open fields. Strong winds push wet, sticky snow along the ground and heap it into balls. When the weather is right, you may see hundreds of snowrollers spread across the open countryside.

Snow Snacks

Just add a few things to some clean snow and have your dessert outside.

What You Need:
clean, fresh snow
cups or bowls — one for each person
spoons — one for each person
powdered juice mix
large mixing bowl
stirring spoon
¾ cup (175 mL) cream
1 cup (250 mL) maple syrup

Snack 1: Sherbet Surprise

1. Spoon some clean snow into each cup. Stir in some juice powder and you have — instant sherbet!

Snack 2: Maple Cream Dream

1. Put some clean snow into the mixing bowl. Pour the cream over the snow.

2. Add the maple syrup, stirring a little as you pour.

3. Spoon out the maple cream snow into cups and serve your friends.

Note: If you live in the city, it is hard to find really clean snow. City air may add harmful chemicals to the snow as it forms and falls. Save this activity for a day in the country.

SOMETHING TO DO

Fake Flakes

Even if you live where it doesn't snow, you can enjoy these six-sided paper flakes.

What You Need:
squares of paper — white or silver
scissors

What to Do:

1. Fold the square of paper on the diagonal. (This means that you make two opposite corners touch — look at Drawings 1 and 2.)

2. Fold again as shown in Drawings 3 and 4.

3. Now cut off the top of the cone you've made, using a zig-zag or wavy line if you like. (Drawing 5.)

4. Make some cuts into the sides of the cone, but don't cut all the way across.

1.

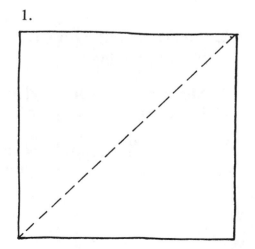

2.

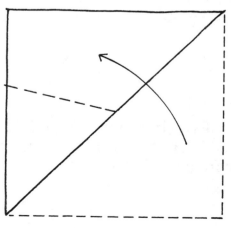

3.

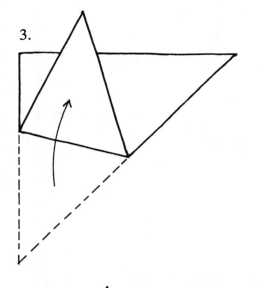

4.

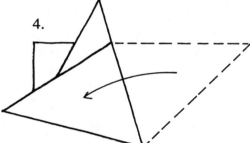

5.

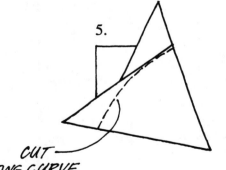

CUT
ALONG CURVE
WITH SCISSORS

5. Unfold and you have a six-sided paper snowflake. (Drawing 8.) You might like to tape your snowflakes to a window as decorations. You can also make small snowflakes to hang on a Christmas tree. Use string or bent paper clips for hangers.

6.

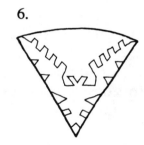

7.

8.

75

The Secret Shapes of Snow

Snow crystals come in many beautiful shapes, but it's hard to see them because they melt so fast. Here's how to take a closer look.

What You Need:
a square of black felt or cardboard,
   about 4 inches x 4 inches (10 cm x 10 cm)
a magnifying glass

What to Do:

1. Take the black square outside. Wait a short time until the square gets cold. (Or put it in the refrigerator for a little while before you go out.)

2. Hold the square out so that a snowflake or two falls on it. Have a look at them through the magnifying glass. Can you see what kinds of crystals make up the snowflake?

3. Collect some more snowflakes. How many different crystal shapes can you find?

4. Try this again on other days. Are the snow crystals different? You might like to keep a notebook about your snow crystals. Make drawings of them or write about how they look. If you have a thermometer, you can record the temperature when you collect your snow crystals. Do different kinds of snow crystals fall when it's very cold? When it's mild?

5. While each snow crystal you see may look a little different from the others, you will probably be able to put it into one of seven groups. (See the chart on p.77.)

Snow crystal names	Shapes
Hexagonal plates	
Stellar crystals	
Hexagonal columns	
Capped columns	
Needles	
Spatial dendrites	
Irregular crystals	

Make Tracks

Out in the woods, you may see tracks left in the snow by a fox or a deer. In the city, you can find the pawprints of cats, dogs, and other animals. Did you know there's a way to take an animal track home with you?

What You Need:
firmly packed snow about 1 inch (at least 3 cm) deep
Note: The temperature must be below freezing. Casting works best when the temperature is between 0°F and 20°F (-18°C and -7°C).

a strip of cardboard, about 5 inches (12 cm)
   wide and 4 or 5 inches (10 to 12 cm) long
a spray bottle filled with water
plaster of Paris (buy at building
   supply or craft store)
a large empty can
1 tsp. (5 mL) salt
stirring spoon or stick
sandpaper

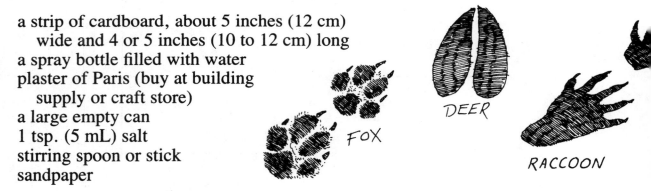

FOX

DEER

RACCOON

What to Do:
1. Find a good clear animal track in the snow.

2. Make the cardboard strip into a ring big enough to fit around the track. Tape the ends of the strip together.

1.

3. Carefully press the cardboard ring into the snow around the track. Leave the ring sticking up a couple of inches (about 5 or 6 cm) out of the snow.

4. Spray the track lightly with water. This will make the track freeze. (You can make a better cast from a hard frozen track.)

5. Pour some water into the can. Stir in plaster of Paris, a little at a time, until the mixture looks like thick, smooth cream.

6. Add 1 teaspoon (5 mL) of salt to the plaster of Paris. This will make it harden faster.

7. Slowly pour the mixture into the cardboard ring.

8. Wait until the plaster is set hard — about 15 to 20 minutes.

9. Take the track out of the snow. Use sandpaper to smooth it.

DOG

CAT

2.

3.

4.

How many different animal tracks can you collect?

Flash and Crash

*I*magine a big old house in the country. Picture it on a sunny day. Then picture it on a stormy night, lit by sudden flashes of lightning. Great claps of thunder echo around its walls. It's quite a different picture now, isn't it?

People who make movies often add thunder and lightning to the scary parts. They know that thunderstorms make people a little nervous. I've always liked thunderstorms, if I can watch them from a safe, dry place. Vancouver, my home city, has very few thunderstorms. But Toronto, where I often work, has 20 to 30 thunderstorm days a year. Most of them are in the summer.

Every minute, about 1,800 thunderstorms are crashing and flashing somewhere in the world. Every minute, about 100 lightning strikes are hitting the earth. Sometimes people say that lightning never strikes twice in the same place. That's not true at all. Toronto's CN Tower, for instance, is hit by lightning up to 70 times a year. Tall buildings like the CN Tower have lightning conductors — metal strips or cables that carry the lightning down to the ground without hurting the building.

Have you ever touched a doorknob and seen a spark snap between your finger and the knob? A flash of lightning is really just a huge spark. The little spark and the great streak of lightning are both sudden flows of electricity. What makes the electricity flow?

Earlier in the book, we talked about molecules — the building blocks of everything in the universe. Molecules are made of even tinier things called *atoms.* For instance, a water molecule is made of two hydrogen atoms and one oxygen atom. Atoms, in turn, have tinier bits in them called *protons* and *electrons.*

Usually, an atom has the same number of protons as it has of electrons. However, if atoms rub together, some of their electrons may be knocked off. These electrons may join other atoms instead. When an atom loses some electrons — so that it ends up with more protons than electrons — it has a *positive electrical charge.* When an atom adds some electrons — so that it ends up with more electrons than protons — it has a *negative electrical charge.*

To see some of the ways atoms behave, you need a couple of balloons, blown up, and a piece of fur. Hang the balloons on strings, side by side. Rub the piece of fur against one of the balloons. Do you hear the electricity crackle? Now hold the piece of fur near the balloon. The balloon swings toward the fur. Here's what's happening. When you rub the fur against the balloon, the fur's atoms lose some of their electrons. They stick to the balloon's atoms instead. The fur becomes positively charged and the balloon becomes negatively charged. Things that have opposite charges *attract* (pull toward) each other.

Next, rub the fur against both balloons. The balloons swing away from each other. Why? Both of the balloons have become negatively charged. Things that have the same charge *repel* (push away) each other.

As you saw, things that have too many electrons are attracted to things that don't have enough. Sometimes, the extra electrons will leap from the negatively charged thing to the positively charged thing. We may see this as a flash of light. And that brings us back to lightning.

Inside big cumulonimbus clouds, strong winds toss raindrops around. As the raindrops collide with each other, some lose atoms and some get extra atoms. The lighter, positively charged drops are swept up to the top of the cloud. Heavier, negatively charged drops gather at the bottom of the cloud. Can you guess what happens next? A huge, sudden spark jumps from one part of the cloud to the other. You may see this as a flickering glow inside the cloud. It's called *sheet lightning*.

You might be surprised to know that, nine times out of ten, lightning happens inside clouds or between clouds. Only about one lightning flash in ten leaps from a cloud to the ground. Lightning zips through the air at over 62,000 miles per second (over 100,000 km per second).

Lightning always takes the easiest path it can find. It is easier for lightning to travel through air that has lots of water in it. Lightning makes zigzags because it is seeking out the wetter parts of the air. If something tall and pointy is handy — a skyscraper, a flagpole, a tall tree — the lightning will go through that instead of the air.

Because lightning is more likely to strike tall things, you should never take shelter under a tree during a storm. If you are out on a baseball field or another flat, open place, *you* may be the tallest thing around. That's why you should go inside when you see a storm coming.

As the lightning streaks to Earth, its path through the air can heat up to 54,000°F (30,000°C). That's almost six times as hot as the surface of the Sun. Do you remember what happens to air when it's heated? Right, it expands (spreads out). The air of the lightning path spreads out so quickly that it sends a huge shock wave through the air around it. This reaches our ears as the crash and rumble of thunder.

Even though thunder and lightning happen at the same time, we see the flash of light first. This is because light reaches our eyes much faster than sound reaches our ears. Light travels at 186,000 miles (300,000 km) per second. Sound travels much more slowly — 1,100 feet (330 m) per second.

Suppose lightning strikes 1.25 miles (2 km) away from you. You'll see the lightning flash a split-second later. You won't hear the thunder for about six seconds — that's time for you to count slowly to six. Although a sudden thunderclap may make you jump, it can't hurt you. In fact, it's telling you about something that's already over!

AMAZING FACTS

The Lightning Man

Ray Sullivan is a retired U.S. national park ranger. He's also a world record holder, although he'd rather not be. He's been struck by lightning seven times, probably more than any other human being. Lightning has given Mr. Sullivan a very rough time. At different times, it has thrown him into the air, knocked him out, hurt his hearing, and torn off one of his toenails. It set his clothing on fire and once even melted his watch. By the way, your chances of being struck by lightning — even once — are very, very low: about 1 in 350,000.

A Shocking Thing to Do

You need dry air to make this work. If your house has a humidifier running, you might ask your parents whether it can be turned off for a day or so.

What You Need:
wool or nylon carpet
a dark room
a metal doorknob
a partner

a dry, cold winter day

What to Do:
1. Stand with your partner in a dark room.

2. Rub your feet on the carpet, back and forth, as fast as you can. Your partner stands still.

3. Now touch your partner. What do you see? What do you feel? (Next, give your partner a chance to rub feet and touch you!)

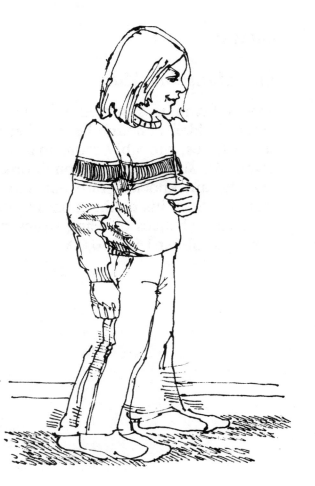

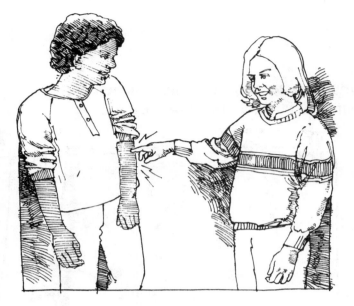

4. Rub your feet on the carpet and touch the metal doorknob. What happens?

5. If both you and your friend rub your feet on the carpet and then touch each other, does anything happen?

What's Happening?
When you rub your feet on the carpet, some of the electrons in the carpet's atoms are rubbed off. They stick to *your* atoms instead, so a negative electrical charge builds up on you. When you touch the doorknob, this electricity is discharged. You feel the shock, and you may see a flash of light. If both you and your friend build up a negative charge, there probably won't be any discharge when you touch each other.

Thunderstorm Countdown

A ligntning flash reaches our eyes much faster than thunder reaches our ears. You can use this fact to figure out how far away the lightning struck.

What to Do:

1. As soon as you see the lightning flash, start counting the seconds like this: one-thousand, two-thousand, three-thousand. . . Stop when you hear thunder.

2. Sound takes about 5 seconds to travel 1 mile (3 seconds to travel 1 km). If you counted to 15, it meant that the lightning was about 3 miles (5 km) away from you.

3. If you count a few thunderclaps like this, you can even tell whether the storm is getting closer to you or moving away.

Great Balls of Kugelblitz

If you ever see a kugelblitz, grab your camera and take a picture. You could be famous. There are only a couple of pictures of what might be ball lightning, and they're not very clear. (*Kugelblitz* is the German word for ball lightning.) In fact, people who study lightning can't agree about what ball lightning is.

Ball lightning is usually seen right after an ordinary lightning flash. It's round or pear-shaped, and about 4 to 8 inches (100 to 200 mm) across. It's about as bright as the lightbulbs in your house. It may glide slowly across a room or sit in one place. Sometimes it seems to explode with a loud popping sound, leaving a bad sulfur smell behind.

Weather Watching

*S*uppose it's a warm, windy spring day. You and a friend are in a basement workshop, making a kite. Your friend says, "Do you think we'll have good kite-flying weather tomorrow?" From a basement workshop, how can you tell what the weather will be tomorrow? The workshop has no windows, so you can't look at the sky. There's no radio or TV, so you can't listen to a forecast.

You think a moment. Then you say, "Maybe tomorrow's weather will be the same as today's." This is a good guess. If you don't have any extra weather information, the best thing to do is expect that tomorrow will be much like today. Weather systems move slowly. Big changes in weather only happen about every three to five days.

Long ago, people didn't know much about big weather systems. They didn't have weather balloons, radar, and weather satellites to watch the weather for them. Today's forecasters use all these things to prepare the weather reports you hear on TV and radio.

Just like you, though, people have always longed to know what kind of weather was on the way. They asked questions like, "Is it safe to plant our beans now, or will a frost kill them? If we take our fishing boats out in the lake tomorrow, will a storm blow up and sink them?"

People hoped they could tell what the weather would be by watching how animals acted. You still hear animal weather sayings today. "If squirrels collect a lot of nuts," some people say, "you can expect a cold winter." Other people who've taken the trouble to study squirrels say this isn't true. Squirrels gather lots of nuts when there are lots of nuts for them to find. This may tell us that a good growing season has gone by, but it doesn't tell us what kind of winter is coming!

Although animals can't tell us what the next season will be like, they may give us some clues to the next few hours' weather. For instance, ants run faster as the air grows hotter, and slow down as the air cools. Many animals become restless and uneasy when a thunderstorm is on the way.

Long ago, people often found that they could foretell the weather by watching the skies. They learned that small puffy white clouds often meant good weather. They noticed that when the wind blew from one direction, it usually brought rain. From another direction, the wind brought hot, dry weather. Some of the sky sayings work quite well. You may have heard this one: "Red sky in the morning, sailor take warning; Red sky at night, sailor's delight."

The sky looks red when the sun is very low in the sky and the air is dry and free of heavy clouds. In most of North America, weather systems move from west to east. If you see a red sky at sunset — in the west — it means that clear weather is on the way. If you see a red sky at sunrise — in the east — it may mean that the good weather has already passed over.

If you know what to look for, you can become skilled at reading the sky too. If you use a notebook to write down what clouds you see each day, and what kind of weather you have, you'll start to see some patterns. You can make some of the weather measuring tools in this book and find out which way (and how hard) the wind is blowing, how much rain is falling, and whether air pressure is rising or falling.

People whose job is forecasting the weather measure all these things, too. Their equipment is much fancier, though, and it gives them more information. They use some of the world's biggest computers to study information that comes in from hundreds of weather stations around the world. They make maps that show the temperatures and winds at the earth's surface and at several levels of the troposphere.

Today's weather forecasters also use photographs taken by satellites. These photographs show large-scale cloud patterns. Forecasters use different types of radar to find out if clouds are raining or snowing. Every day, new equipment is being developed to help people who study weather make better and better forecasts. Hundreds of lives can be saved if people can be warned to get away or take shelter before a hurricane hits — or a tornado, or a blizzard.

Countries often keep secrets from each other. However, all the world's countries share weather information. They know how important it is to air travellers, sailors, farmers . . . and kite-flyers like you and me!

AMAZING FACTS

Can Jet Planes Change the Weather?

Chicago, Illinois has the busiest airport in the world. A plane is taking off or landing about every 42 seconds, around the clock. American weather scientists have noticed that the weather around Chicago has become cloudier and rainier in recent years. They think planes may be causing this. How? The exhaust from plane engines puts a lot of water vapor into the sky. The water vapor condenses in the cold air to make a *contrail*. A contrail is the long thin cloud that you often see trailing behind a plane. Where there are many planes, the contrails can join together to make sheets of cirrus cloud. These block the sun and may bring cooler rainier weather to Chicago.

The Cricket Weather Report

Want to know the temperature? The crickets will tell you.

What You Need:
a summer night when crickets are singing
a watch
pencil and paper
an outdoor thermometer, so that you can check your result

What to Do:

1. Cricket chirps are a familiar sound on late summer nights. Try to count the number of chirps you hear in 15 seconds. Use a watch so that you'll know when 15 seconds are up. Sometimes it's not easy to decide when one chirp ends and another begins. Give it a few tries.

2. First, let's find the temperature in Fahrenheit. Take the number of cricket chirps in 15 seconds. Add 40. The number you get is the temperature in Fahrenheit. (Your answer should be within a couple of degrees of the actual temperature. Use a thermometer to check.) For example, suppose you heard 36 chirps in 15 seconds.
36 + 40 = 76
The temperature is about 76°F.

3. If you would like to find the temperature in Celsius, do this. Take the number of cricket chirps in 15 seconds. Divide this number by 2. Then add 6. The number you get is the temperature in Celsius. For example, suppose you heard 36 chirps in 15 seconds.
36 ÷ 2 = 18
18 + 6 = 24.
The temperature is about 24°C.

Track Down Some Microclimates

Have you ever read one of those stories about a haunted house with a "cold spot"? Well, every house has cold spots — and warm ones, windy ones, damp ones, and dry ones. Microclimates are the climates of small areas. You can go looking for some in your house.

What You Need:
thermometer
tissue or tissue paper
pencil or stick
clear sticky tape

What to Do:

1. **Sunny Places.** Which places in your house are sunny in the morning? In the afternoon? Which seems a warmer place to stand — beside a window with morning sun coming in, or beside a window with afternoon sun? Is the temperature higher next to a sunny window than in the middle of a room? Use your thermometer to measure the temperature in different places.

2. **Dust.** In sunbeams you can often see bits of dust spinning crazily. A little gust of wind is tossing them around. Can you see any pattern to the movements of the dust? Are the bits going up? Down? Put your hand into the sunbeam and twirl your hand in tight circles. What happens to the dust?

Dust is so light that even the slightest breeze picks it up. So dust collects only where it is very still. Where do the "dust bunnies" gather in your house?

3. **Winds.** Make a draft detector: Tape one edge of a tissue or a small piece of tissue paper to a pencil. Blow on it to make sure it moves easily. Now take it around the house. Are there any drafts coming in around doors and windows? This is easier to check on a cold day. As warm air rises in your house, cold air will rush in under doors and windowsills to replace it. Ask if you can try your draft detector on the refrigerator. Open the refrigerator door while holding your draft meter at the top of the door. What happens? Close the door. Now open it again, holding the draft detector at the bottom. Which way does it blow? Can you explain what's happening?

4. **Damp or Dry?** Is it humid or dry in your house? Signs of humidity:
   (1) drawers and doors that stick (wood takes in water vapor and swells)

(2) peeling paint; wallpaper pulling away from wall
(3) condensation on inside of windows (cold weather)
(4) mold and mildew — look for black or grey spots on bathroom walls or between tiles

Signs of dryness:
(1) dry inside of nose when you wake up
(2) cracking plaster and cracking wood furniture
(3) getting a shock when you touch a doorknob or light switch
(4) long hair crackling when you comb it

Groundhog Daze

February 2 is Groundhog Day. According to the old story, if a groundhog sees its shadow at noon on that day, we'll have six more weeks of winter. A man named Reuben Hornstein decided to see if this was true. He looked at 10 years of Toronto weather records. In three of those years, February 2 was cloudy. This means the groundhog *couldn't* see its shadow. But was winter over any earlier than usual? Nope. There were seven years with sunny Groundhog Days. But four of these years had much milder, shorter winters than usual. The groundhog story was right for the other three years, when winter dragged on. So the groundhog scored only three out of 10 — at least in Toronto. By the way, in Europe hundreds of years ago, people used hedgehogs to predict the end of winter. But when European settlers first came to Canada, they couldn't find any of these spiny little critters. So they gave the poor groundhog the forecasting job.

Index

CHICAGO HEIGHTS PUBLIC LIBRARY

CHICAGO HEIGHTS FREE PUBLIC LIBRARY

3 239 00154 9273

95, 98, 00, 03, 09

j-551.5
S968L
Suzuki, David
Looking at weather
c.1

CHICAGO HEIGHTS FREE PUBLIC LIBRARY
15TH ST. & CHICAGO ROAD
CHICAGO HEIGHTS, ILL.
60411
PHONE: (708) 754-0323

GAYLORD S